STANDARD OF EXCELLENCE

FIRST PERFORMANCE

13 Pieces in a Variety of Styles for Beginning Band

BY BRUCE PEARSON & BARRIE GOTT

Dear Student:

Welcome to the STANDARD OF EXCELLENCE FIRST PERFORMANCE, a collection of thirteen songs written for beginning or young band. These selections represent a variety of musical styles such as rock, blues, marches, traditional folk songs, and transcriptions from classical music.

Each piece was composed or arranged especially for the first year band student and contains a limited range of musical notes as well as simple rhythms designed to provide beginning instrumentalists a repertoire of varied fun and exciting concert music.

Good luck with your First Performance!

Best wishes,

Bruce Pearson

Bruce Pearson

Barrie Gott

Barrie Gott

ISBN 0-8497-0659-9

 NEIL A. KJOS MUSIC COMPANY • PUBLISHER

A Children's Christmas Carol
"O Come, Little Children"

1st B♭ Trumpet/Cornet

J.A.P. Schulz/Magill

A Children's Christmas Carol
"O Come, Little Children"

2nd B♭ Trumpet/Cornet

J.A.P. Schulz/Magill

O Come, Little Children was composed by Johann Abraham Peter Schulz (b.1747 - d.1800). Schulz was the court composer at Rheinsberg, Germany and a choir director for the Royal Court Theater in Copenhagen, Denmark. He was best known for setting poems to simple, folk-like music. The German poet, Christoph von Schmid, wrote the words to this song.

THE FRIENDLY BEASTS

1st B♭ Trumpet/Cornet

Medieval French Melody

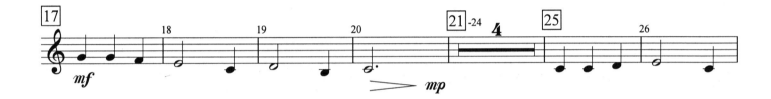

THE FRIENDLY BEASTS

2nd B♭ Trumpet/Cornet

Medieval French Melody

The melody for **The Friendly Beasts** dates back to 12th century medieval France while the words were written at a later date. **The Friendly Beasts** is usually thought of as an old English carol.

RIO BRAVO

1st B♭ Trumpet/Cornet

RIO BRAVO

2nd B♭ Trumpet/Cornet

Latin America is made up of South America, Central America, Mexico, and the West Indies. The music of this region is a combination of Spanish, Portuguese, and Italian traditions and has been influenced by the cultures of the native Indians like the Aztec, Incan, and Mayan. It features catchy melodies, infectious rhythms, and a wide use of percussion instruments.

W26TP

BIG ROCK CANDY MOUNTAIN

1st B♭ Trumpet/Cornet

Traditional American Folk

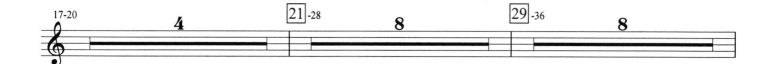

W26TP

BIG ROCK CANDY MOUNTAIN

2nd B♭ Trumpet/Cornet

Traditional American Folk

Folk songs are passed down from generation to generation through singing and listening. The common folk sing the songs to their children instead of writing them down. The original composers were forgotten as time passed and the words and places changed. These changes left many versions of the same song. **Big Rock Candy Mountain** originated in the late 1800's and was attributed to Harry "Haywire Mac" McClintock. The ballad tells of a hobo's life, riding the trains and traveling the country, in search of the perfect place for a "burly bum" to live.

ROYAL CROWN MARCH

1st B♭ Trumpet/Cornet

ROYAL CROWN MARCH

2nd B♭ Trumpet/Cornet

The history of the march has its beginnings in the military. Marches have a steady beat that is strongly accented. This beat was helpful for soldiers to stay in step. Many marches were written to commemorate a regal occasion such as the crowning of a king. It was with this in mind that **Royal Crown March** was composed.

W26TP

Boot Scootin' Barn Dance

Ron Cowherd
Traditional American Folk

1st B♭ Trumpet/Cornet

W26TP

BOOT SCOOTIN' BARN DANCE

Ron Cowherd
Traditional American Folk

2nd Bb Trumpet/Cornet

A significant part of a country's heritage and culture is found in its folk music. Using the language of the common folk, folk songs describe the lives and times of its people. This piece uses the folk song, **Ol' Joe Clark.** Joe Clark was a veteran from the war of 1812 who lived in the Appalachian Mountains. The numerous verses were made up from incidents in his life and expanded as time passed to include over 90 different verses.

Bag O' Blues

1st B♭ Trumpet/Cornet

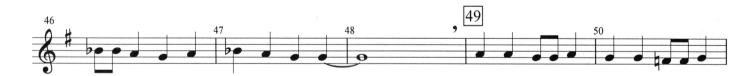

BAG O' BLUES

2nd B♭ Trumpet/Cornet

The blues is a style of music developed from the African-American field hollers, work songs, and spirituals of the late 1800's to early 1900's. It is played at a slow to moderate tempo and usually written in 4/4 time. The third, fifth, and seventh notes of the scale in which the piece is written are lowered one half-step.

W26TP

A LITTLE BIT OF LATIN

1st B♭ Trumpet/Cornet

A Little Bit of Latin

2nd B♭ Trumpet/Cornet

The music of Latin America, influenced by the many cultures and traditions of its people, uses lively rhythms for dances like the habanera, rumba, cha-cha, and tango. The music uses many percussion instruments such as the claves, maracas, and cowbell to keep the rhythm.

A Classical Canon

1st B♭ Trumpet/Cornet

Franz Joseph Haydn/Magill

10

A Classical Canon

2nd B♭ Trumpet/Cornet

Franz Joseph Haydn/Magill

Franz Joseph Haydn (b.1732 - d.1809) was an Austrian composer who worked as the court composer for the royal Esterhazy family for over thirty years. "Papa Haydn," best known for his numerous symphonies and string quartets, also trained and conducted the other court musicians. **A Classical Canon** was originally called the *Nightingale Canon*. Words were added later describing children's anticipation to stay up on Christmas Eve while the parent sang for the children to go to bed. The title then became commonly known as the *Christmas Eve Canon*.

Dr. Rock

1st B♭ Trumpet/Cornet

Chuck Elledge

DR. ROCK

2nd B♭ Trumpet/Cornet

Chuck Elledge

Rock music evolved into a distinctive style of music with songs like *Rock Around the Clock* and *You Ain't Nothin' But a Hound Dog*. During the 1960's, a British band called the Beatles became very popular. In the 1970's and 1980's, electronic instruments and advanced recording techniques were developed to enhance the music.

FANFARE AND MINUET FROM
"THE ROYAL FIREWORKS"

1st B♭ Trumpet/Cornet

George Frideric Handel

FANFARE AND MINUET FROM
"THE ROYAL FIREWORKS"

2nd B♭ Trumpet/Cornet

George Frideric Handel

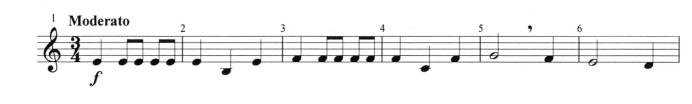

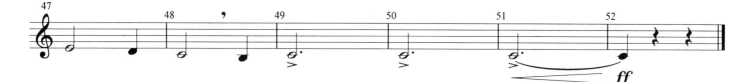

George Frideric Handel (b.1685 - d.1759) was a popular German composer who traveled widely throughout his life and settled in England. The English royalty paid him well for his many compositions. The **Music for the Royal Fireworks**, written in 1749, originally called for a huge ensemble of brass, woodwinds, timpani, and a cannon. Handel wrote the piece to accompany a fireworks celebration for the King of England. Just as the music began, a whole box of fireworks exploded by accident. Handel's piece, however, was a great success.

BOOGIE BLUES

1st B♭ Trumpet/Cornet

BOOGIE BLUES

2nd B♭ Trumpet/Cornet

Blues music evolved throughout the early 20th century. "Boogie-woogie," a popular style developed during this time, was normally played at a fast tempo, had a repeated melodic pattern in the bass (called a "walking bass"), swinging eighth notes, and a series of improvised variations in the upper melody.

MINOR ROCK

1st B♭ Trumpet/Cornet

MINOR ROCK

2nd B♭ Trumpet/Cornet

"Rock and Roll" was a phrase used by disk jockey, Allan Freed, in the early 1950's. He wanted to attract teenagers to his Rhythm and Blues concerts. The name caught on and rock and roll replaced American "pop" music. Rock music has a heavy dance beat with strong accents on beats 2 and 4 and lyrics that relate well to young people.

W26TP

GLOSSARY

Accent > .... play the beginning of the note louder

Accidentals ♯, ♭, ♮ .... sharp, flat, or natural

Allegro .... quick and lively

Andante .... moderately slow

Articulation .... type of attack used to play a note or group of notes

Bar Line .... divides the music staff into measures

Bass Clef .... F Clef, read by bassoon, trombone, baritone, tuba, timpani, and electric bass

Blues .... American genre of popular vocal music, developed from African-American field hollers, work songs, and spirituals; characterized by a harmonic structure that is made up of a 12-measure phrase

Breath Mark ' .... take a breath

Canon .... a style of contrapuntal music, similar to a round

Carol .... song usually associated with Christmas

Common Time C .... same as 4/4

Crescendo .... gradually play louder

Decrescendo .... gradually play softer

Double Bar .... marks the end of the music

Dynamics .... loudness or softness of music

Fermata .... hold note or rest longer than its usual value

Flat ♭ .... lowers the pitch of a note by a half step

Forte *f* .... loud

Fortissimo *ff* .... very loud

Harmony .... result of two or more different notes played or sung at the same time

Improvise .... to create music as it is being performed

Jazz .... style of American popular music that emerged at the turn of the 20th century and continued to evolve throughout the 20th century

Key Signature .... sharps or flats stated right after the clef; key signatures change certain notes throughout a piece of music

Ledger Lines .... short lines added above or below the staff used to extend the staff to notate pitches that are beyond the range of the staff

Long Rest .... rest the number of measures indicated

Maestoso .... majestically

Measure .... space between two bar lines; also known as a "bar"

Medieval .... (also known as Middle Ages, 400-1400AD) a time in European history of warfare, religious devotion, and royal pageantry

Melody .... organized succession of tones

Mezzo Forte *mf* .... medium loud

Mezzo Piano *mp* .... medium soft

Moderato .... moderate speed

Natural ♮ .... cancels a flat or sharp

One-Measure Repeat ✕ ...... repeat the previous measure

Percussion Clef .... indicates that the lines and spaces on the staff do not designate specific pitches; also called neutral clef or no-pitch clef; read by snare drum, bass drum, cymbals, and most other auxiliary percussion instruments

Phrase .... musical thought or sentence

Piano *p* .... soft

Pick-Up Note(s) .... note or notes that come before the first full measure of a piece

Popular Music .... music of everyday life, it has played a role in each historical period

Repeat Sign .... repeat from beginning or repeat the section of music between repeat signs

Rhythm and Blues .... American style of popular music often described as an urban style of blues; instrumentation included drums, piano, electric guitar and bass, saxophone, brass, and vocalists

Rock .... style of American popular music that developed in the 1960's from rock and roll, with more amplification and distortion of sound and more room for improvisation

Rock and Roll .... style of American popular music that developed from rhythm and blues in the 1950's and was especially popular among young people

Sharp ♯ .... raises the pitch of a note 1/2 step

Slur .... curved line connecting two or more notes of <u>different</u> pitches

Solo/Soli .... one person plays/whole section plays

Staccato .... dot placed above or below a note meaning to play short and detached

Staff .... lines and spaces on which music is written

Swing .... style of American popular music that was played by the "big bands" of the 1930's and 1940's

Tempo .... speed of music

Tenuto .... line placed above or below a note meaning to sustain for full value

Tie .... curved line that connects two notes on the <u>same</u> line or space

Time Signature 4/4 3/4 2/4 .... top number tells the number of counts in each measure; bottom number tells the type of note that receives one count

Treble Clef .... G Clef; read by flute, oboe, clarinets, saxophones, trumpet, French horn, and mallet percussion

Two-Measure Repeat .... repeat the two previous measures